What a Waste

words by Jill McDougall
photographs by Martin Smith

We use lots of water every day. We use water for drinking and washing. We use water in our garden. There are many ways we can save water.

3

This boy is cleaning the path. What a waste! He could save water if he used a broom.

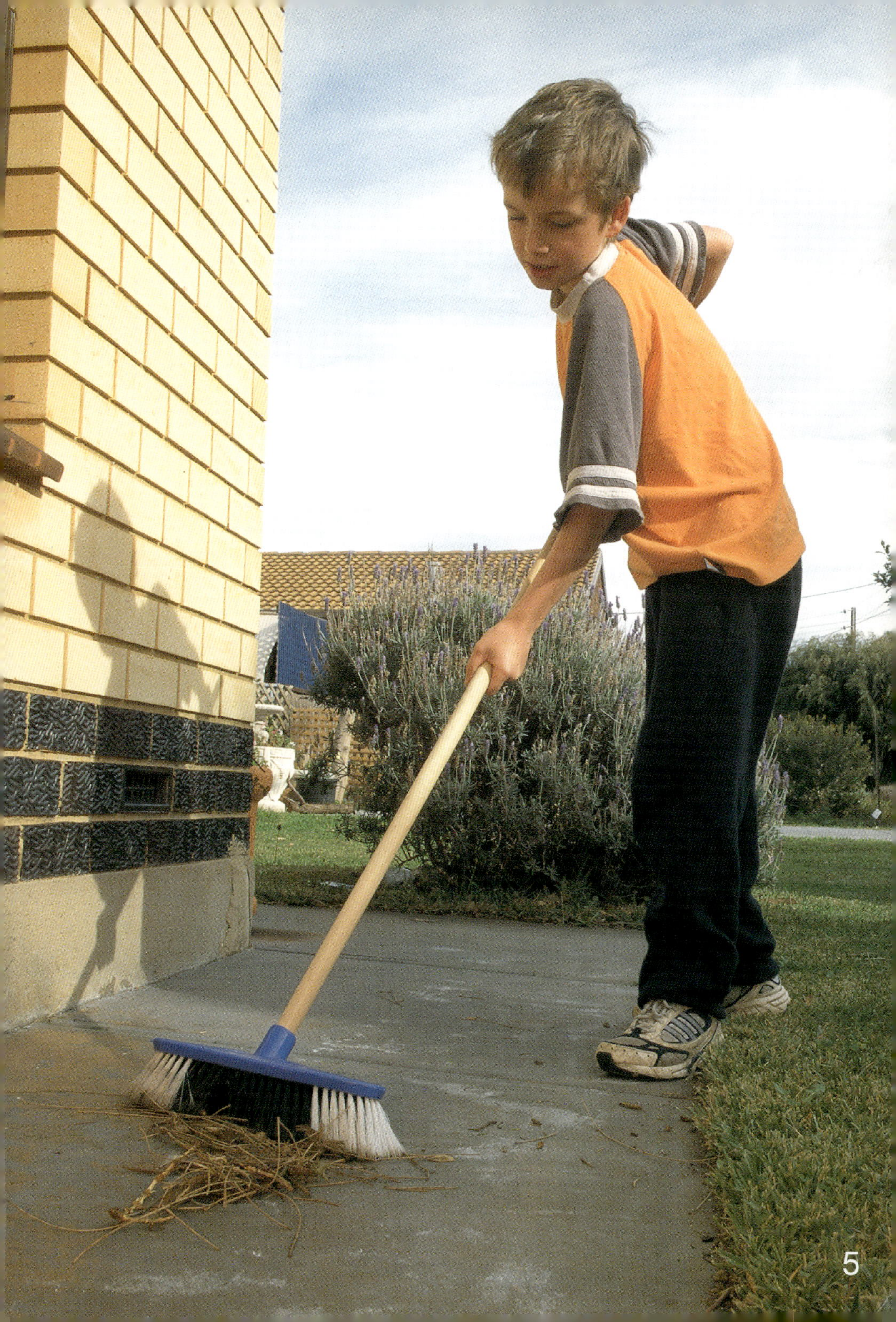

This girl is cleaning her teeth. She has left the water running. What a waste! She could save water if she turned it off.

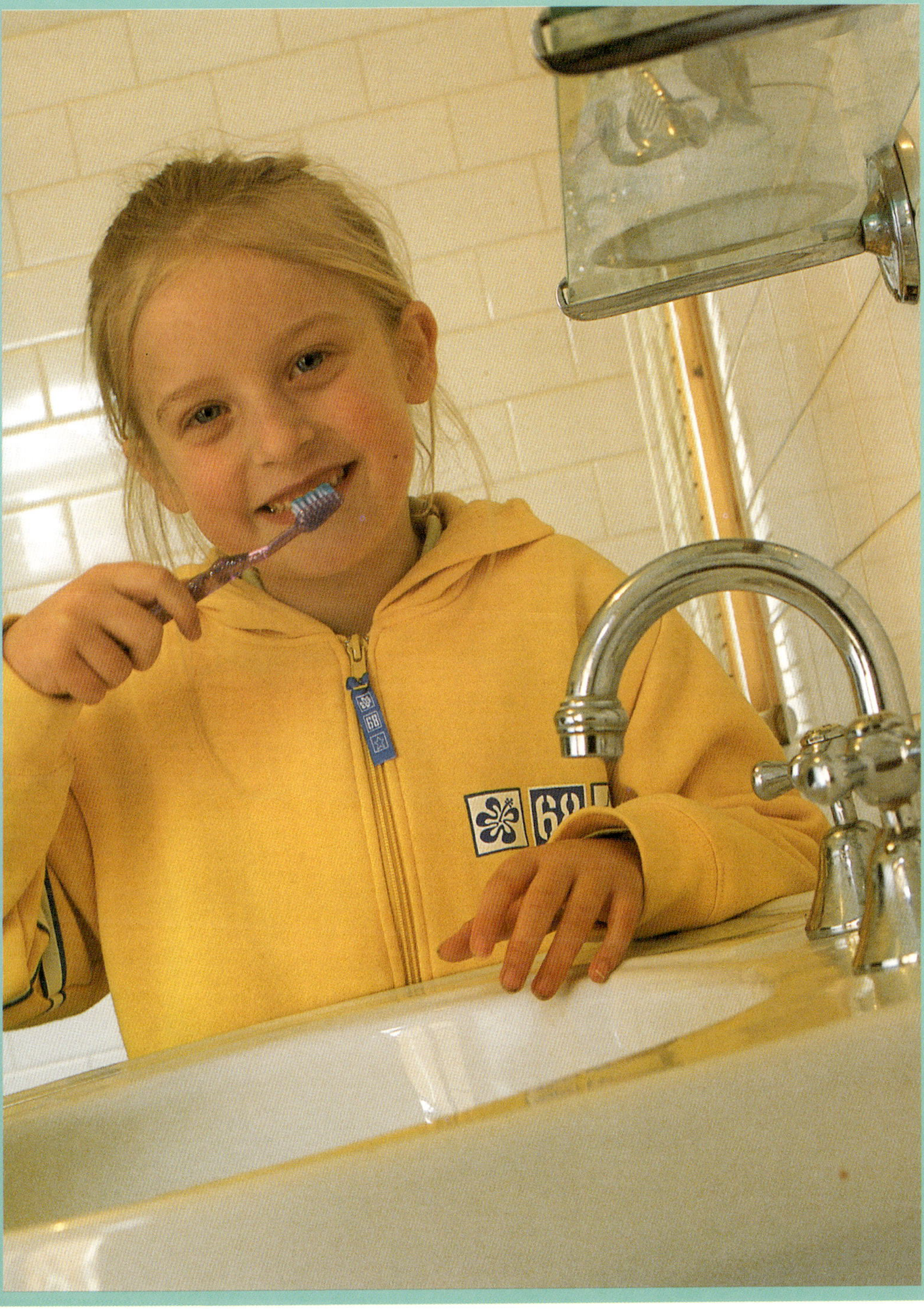

This man is watering his garden. The water is running down the street. What a waste! The man could save water if he moved the hose.

9

This woman is washing her car. What a waste! She could save water if she used a bucket.

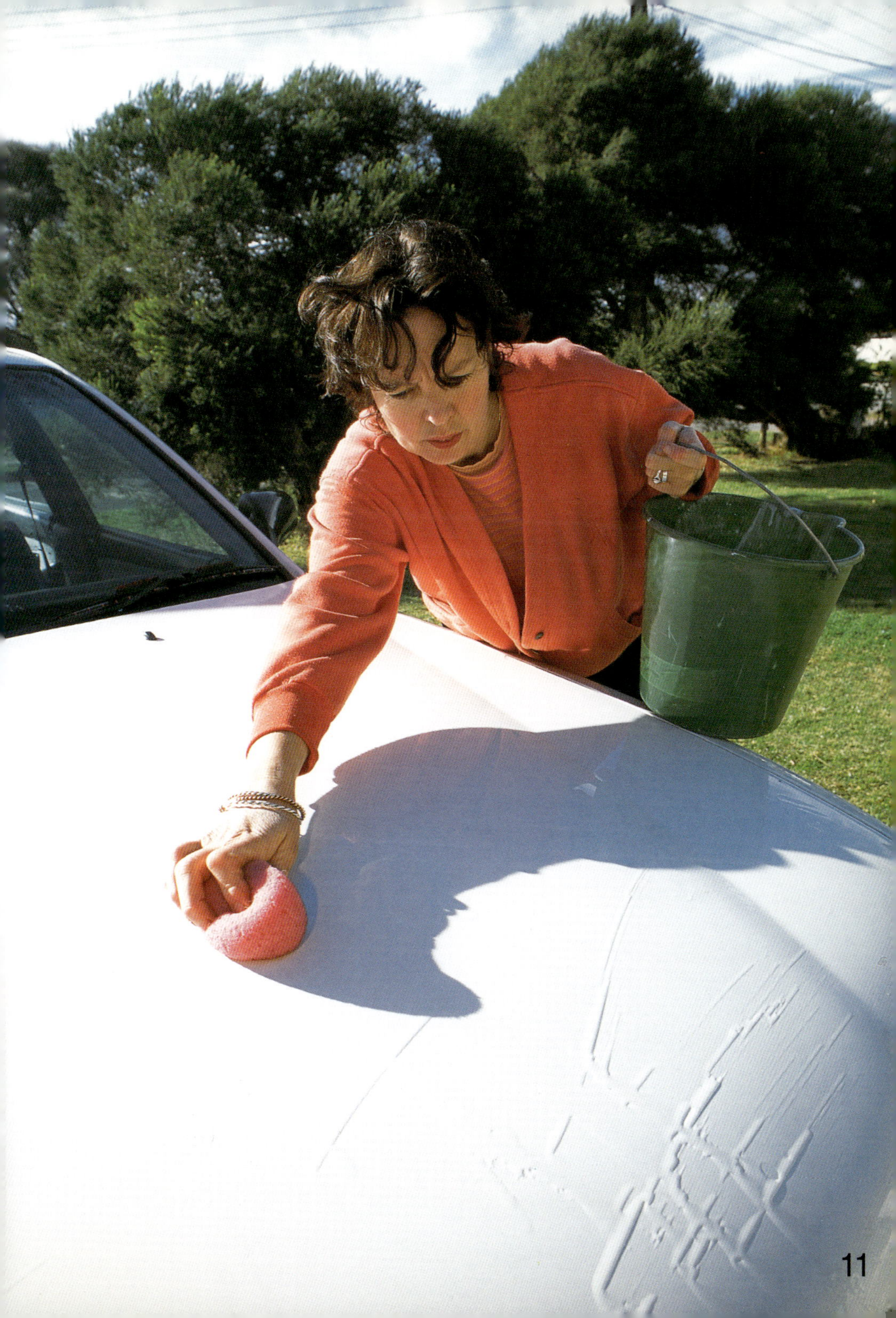

This girl wants a drink. She is waiting for the water to cool down. What a waste! She could save water if she kept some in the fridge.

13

This boy has some dirty water. He gives it to the plants. Is this a waste? No. It is a good way to save water.

15

We need water to live. We must be careful not to waste it.